BIG-NOTE PIANO
ESSENTIAL CLASSICAL

ISBN 978-0-634-09362-3

HAL•LEONARD®
CORPORATION
7777 W. BLUEMOUND RD. P.O. BOX 13819
MILWAUKEE, WISCONSIN 53213

In Australia Contact:
Hal Leonard Australia Pty. Ltd.
4 Lentara Court
Cheltenham, Victoria, 3192 Australia
Email: ausadmin@halleonard.com

Visit Hal Leonard Online at
www.halleonard.com

AVE MARIA

By FRANZ SCHUBERT

BARCAROLLE
from THE TALES OF HOFFMANN

Gently and quietly, but not too slow

By JACQUES OFFENBACH

BLUE DANUBE WALTZ

Music by JOHANN STRAUSS, JR.

CAN CAN
from ORPHEUS IN THE UNDERWORLD

By JACQUES OFFENBACH

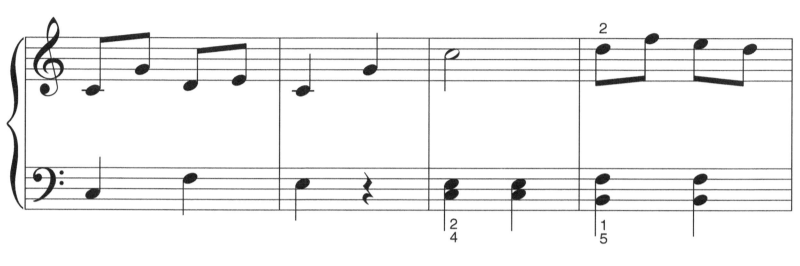

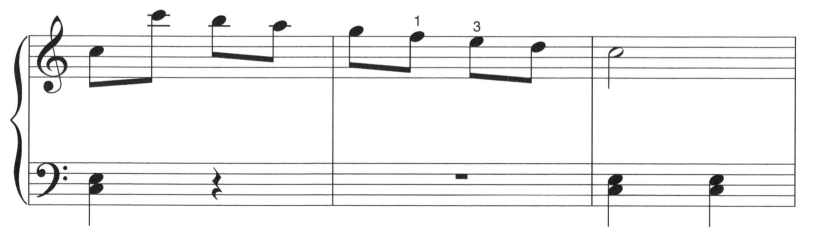

HABANERA
from CARMEN

By GEORGES BIZET

CARNIVAL OF VENICE

By JULIUS BENEDICT

FÜR ELISE

By LUDWIG VAN BEETHOVEN

Gently, moderately slow

Ped. simile

HUMORESQUE

By ANTONÍN DVORÁK

MINUET IN G
from the ANNA MAGDALENA NOTEBOOK

By JOHANN SEBASTIAN BACH

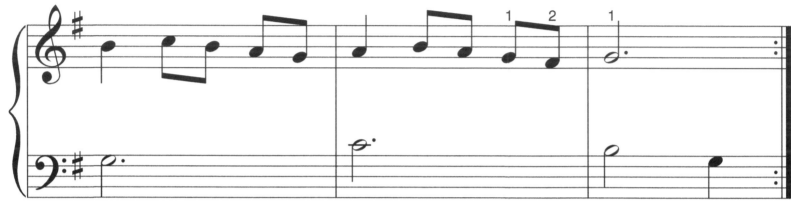

JESU, JOY OF MAN'S DESIRING

By JOHANN SEBASTIAN BACH

Calmly (each measure = 1 slow beat)

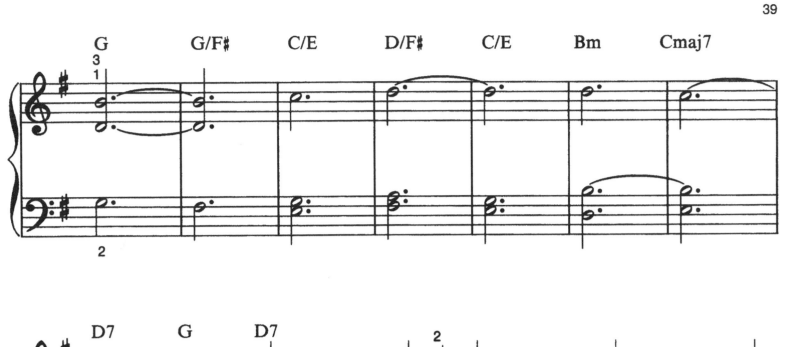

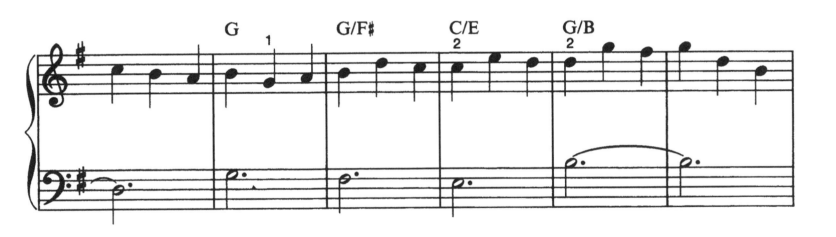

LA DONNA È MOBILE

from RIGOLETTO

By GIUSEPPE VERDI

LARGO
from XERXES

By GEORGE FRIDERIC HANDEL

Slowly and solemnly

With pedal

MORNING
from PEER GYNT

By EDVARD GRIEG

Moderately

With pedal

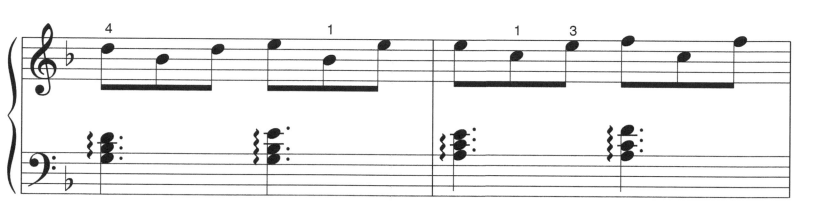

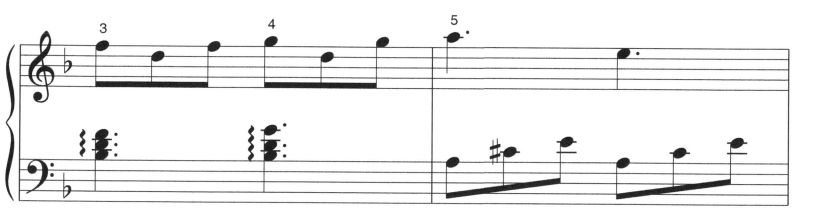

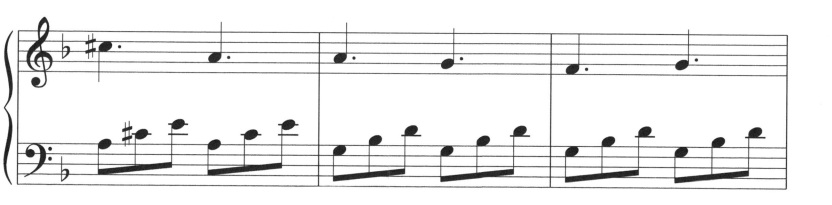

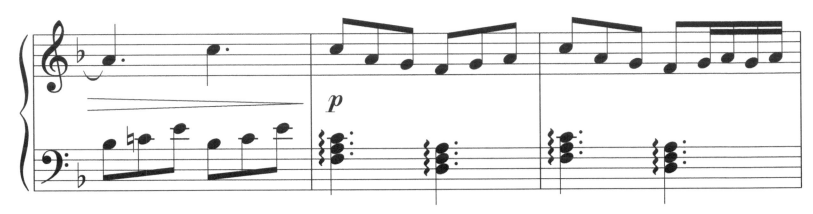

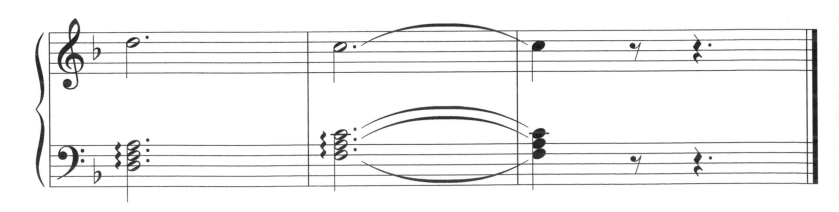

ODE TO JOY
from SYMPHONY NO. 9 IN D MINOR, FOURTH MOVEMENT CHORAL THEME

Words by HENRY VAN DYKE
Music by LUDWIG VAN BEETHOVEN

PAVANE

By GABRIEL FAURÉ

54

D.S. al Coda

CODA

PIANO CONCERTO NO. 21

("Elvira Madigan")
Second Movement Excerpt

By WOLFGANG AMADEUS MOZART

POMP AND CIRCUMSTANCE

Words by ARTHUR BENSON
Music by EDWARD ELGAR

Slow march, in 2 (♩ = 1 beat)

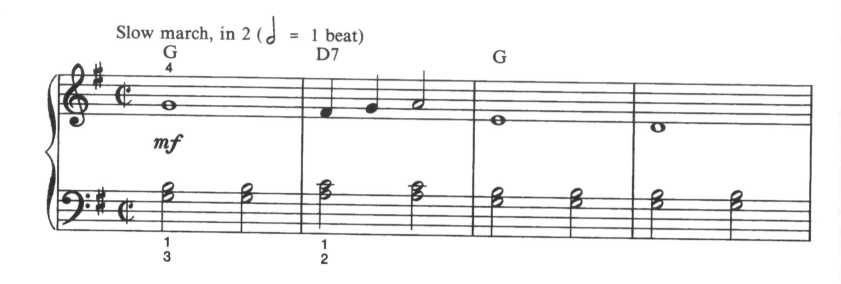

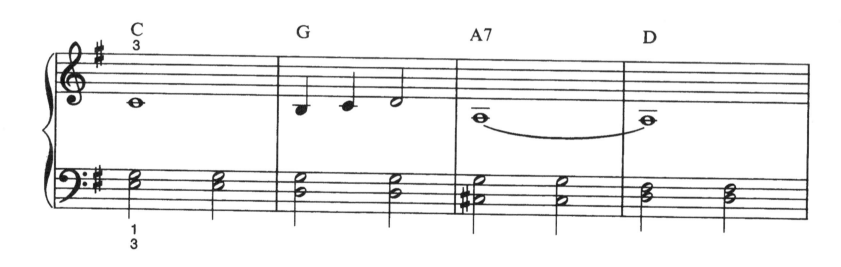

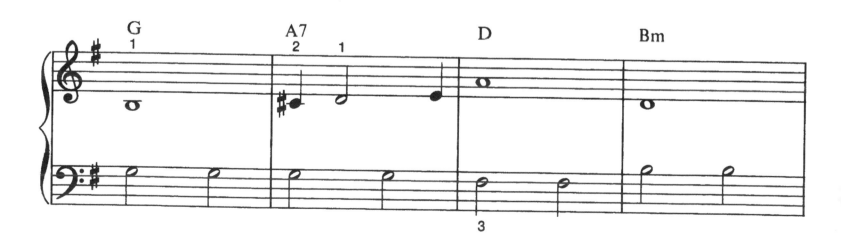

THE SLEEPING BEAUTY WALTZ

By PYOTR IL'YICH TCHAIKOVSKY

SYMPHONY NO. 40
First Movement Excerpt

By WOLFGANG AMADEUS MOZART

SYMPHONY NO. 5
First Movement Excerpt

By LUDWIG VAN BEETHOVEN

Majestically

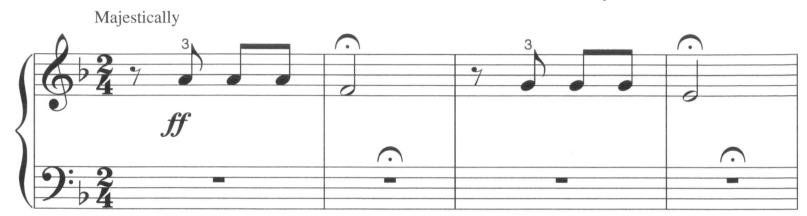

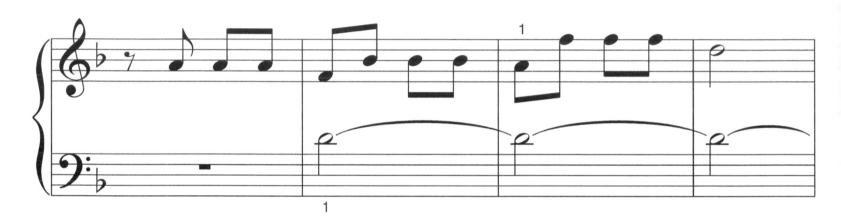

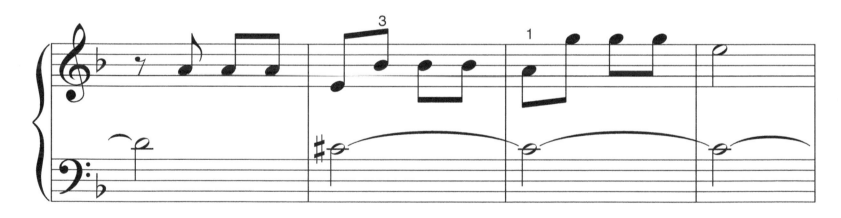

SYMPHONY NO. 9

("From the New World")
Second Movement Excerpt

By ANTONÍN DVOŘÁK

Slowly

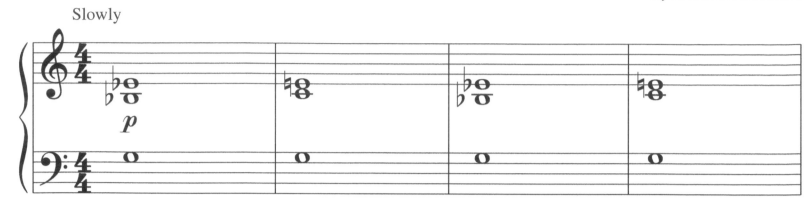

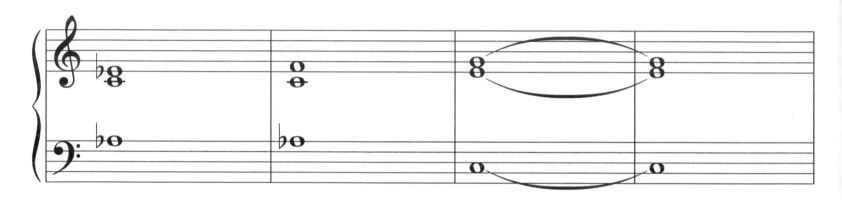

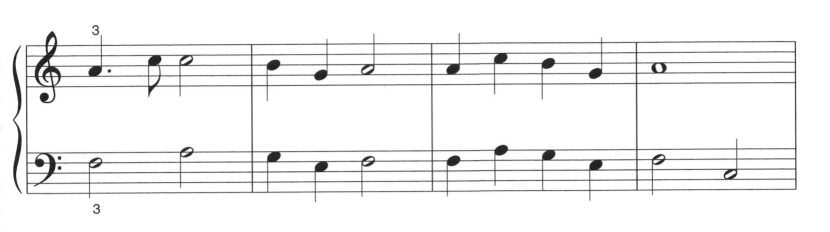

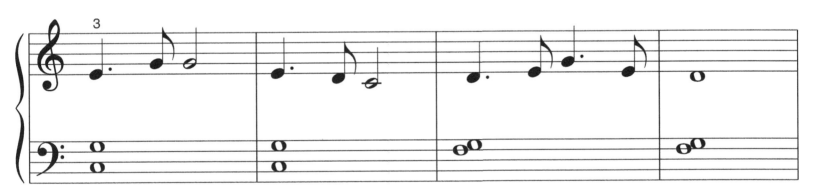

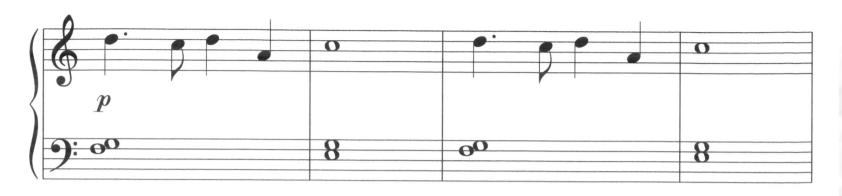

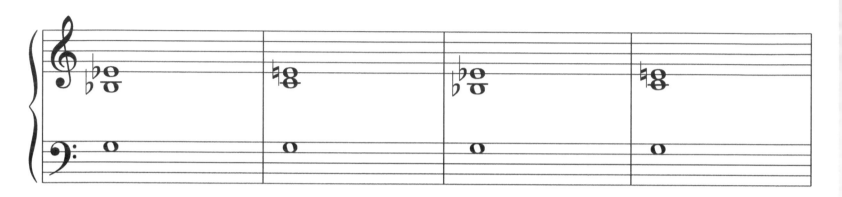

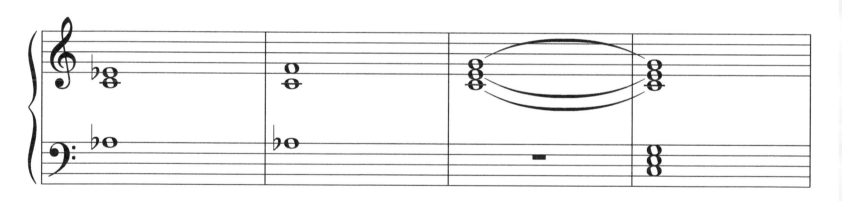

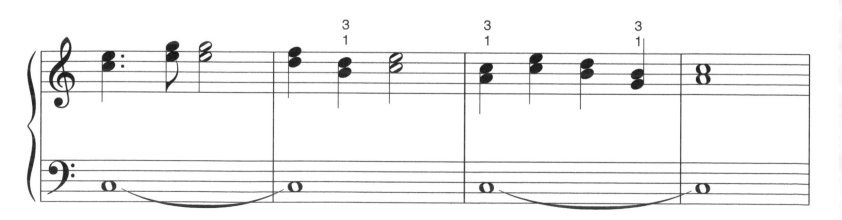

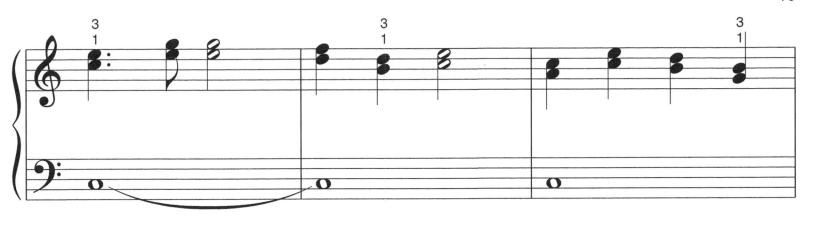

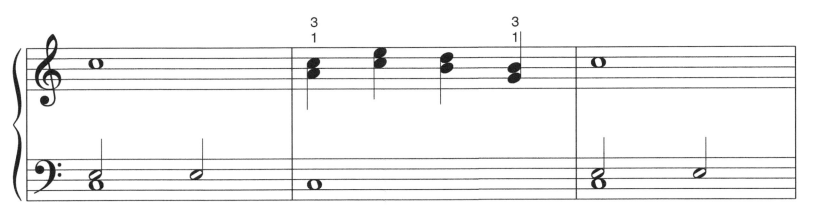

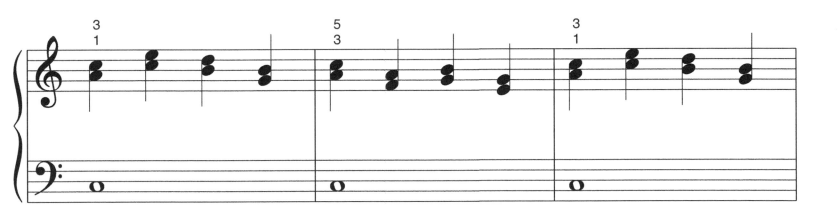

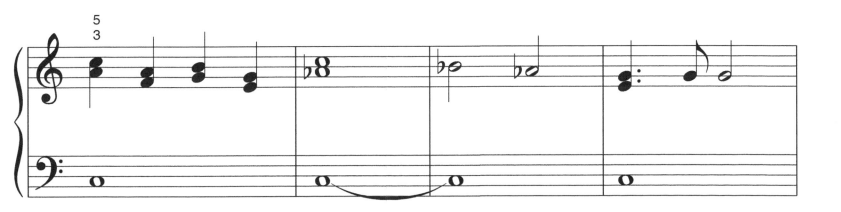

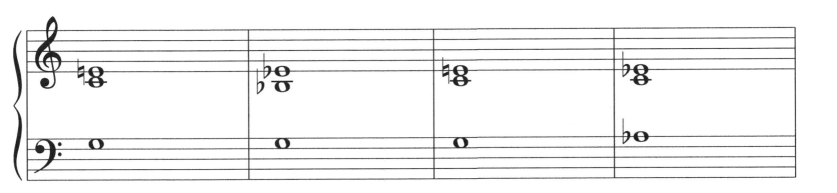

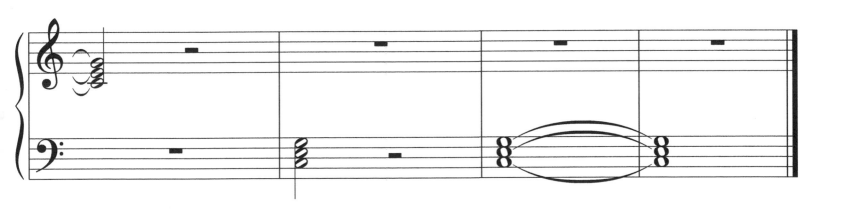

TRIUMPHAL MARCH
from AÏDA

By GIUSEPPE VERDI

Big Fun with Big-Note Piano Books!

These songbooks feature exciting easy arrangements for beginning piano students.

Best of Adele
Now even beginners can play their favorite Adele tunes! This book features big-note arrangements of 10 top songs: Chasing Pavements • Daydreamer • Hometown Glory • Lovesong • Make You Feel My Love • One and Only • Rolling in the Deep • Set Fire to the Rain • Someone like You • Turning Tables.
00308601 ....$14.99

Beatles' Best
27 classics for beginners to enjoy, including: Can't Buy Me Love • Eleanor Rigby • Hey Jude • Michelle • Here, There and Everywhere • When I'm Sixty-Four • Yesterday • and more.
00222561..$14.99

The Best Songs Ever
70 favorites, featuring: Body and Soul • Crazy • Edelweiss • Fly Me to the Moon • Georgia on My Mind • Imagine • The Lady Is a Tramp • Memory • A String of Pearls • Tears in Heaven • Unforgettable • You Are So Beautiful • and more.
00310425 ....$19.95

Children's Favorite Movie Songs
arranged by Phillip Keveren
16 favorites from films, including: The Bare Necessities • Beauty and the Beast • Can You Feel the Love Tonight • Do-Re-Mi • The Rainbow Connection • Tomorrow • Zip-A-Dee-Doo-Dah • and more.
00310838 ....$12.99

Classical Music's Greatest Hits
24 beloved classical pieces, including: Air on the G String • Ave Maria • By the Beautiful Blue Danube • Canon in D • Eine Kleine Nachtmusik • Für Elise • Ode to Joy • Romeo and Juliet • Waltz of the Flowers • more.
00310475 ....$12.99

Disney Big-Note Collection
Over 40 Disney favorites, including: Circle of Life • Colors of the Wind • Hakuna Matata • It's a Small World • Under the Sea • A Whole New World • Winnie the Pooh • Zip-A-Dee-Doo-Dah • and more.
00316056..$19.99

Essential Classical
22 simplified piano pieces from top composers, including: Ave Maria (Schubert) • Blue Danube Waltz (Strauss) • Für Elise (Beethoven) • Jesu, Joy of Man's Desiring (Bach) • Morning (Grieg) • Pomp and Circumstance (Elgar) • and many more.
00311205..$10.99

Favorite Children's Songs
arranged by Bill Boyd
29 easy arrangements of songs to play and sing with children: Peter Cottontail • I Whistle a Happy Tune • It's a Small World • On the Good Ship Lollipop • The Rainbow Connection • and more!
00240251..$12.99

Frozen
9 songs from this hit Disney film, plus full-color illustrations from the movie. Songs include the standout single "Let It Go", plus: Do You Want to Build a Snowman? • For the First Time in Forever • Reindeer(s) Are Better Than People • and more.
00126105 ....$12.99

Happy Birthday to You and Other Great Songs for Big-Note Piano
16 essential favorites, including: Chitty Chitty Bang Bang • Good Night • Happy Birthday to You • Heart and Soul • Over the Rainbow • Sing • This Land Is Your Land • and more.
00119636 ....$9.99

Elton John – Greatest Hits
20 of his biggest hits, including: Bennie and the Jets • Candle in the Wind • Crocodile Rock • Rocket Man • Tiny Dancer • Your Song • and more.
00221832..$14.99

Les Misérables
14 favorites from the Broadway sensation arranged for beginning pianists. Titles include: At the End of the Day • Bring Him Home • Castle on a Cloud • I Dreamed a Dream • In My Life • On My Own • Who Am I? • and more.
00221812 ....$15.99

The Phantom of the Opera
9 songs from the Broadway spectacular, including: All I Ask of You • Angel of Music • Masquerade • The Music of the Night • The Phantom of the Opera • The Point of No Return • Prima Donna • Think of Me • Wishing You Were Somehow Here Again.
00110006 ....$14.99

Pride & Prejudice
Music from the Motion Picture Soundtrack
12 piano pieces from the 2006 Oscar-nominated film: Another Dance • Darcy's Letter • Georgiana • Leaving Netherfield • Liz on Top of the World • Meryton Townhall • The Secret Life of Daydreams • Stars and Butterflies • and more.
00316125 ....$12.99

The Sound of Music
arranged by Phillip Keveren
9 favorites: Climb Ev'ry Mountain • Do-Re-Mi • Edelweiss • The Lonely Goatherd • Maria • My Favorite Things • Sixteen Going on Seventeen • So Long, Farewell • The Sound of Music.
00316057..$10.99

Best of Taylor Swift
A dozen top tunes from this crossover sensation: Fearless • Fifteen • Hey Stephen • Love Story • Our Song • Picture to Burn • Teardrops on My Guitar • White Horse • You Belong with Me • and more.
00307143 ....$12.99

Worship Favorites
20 powerful songs: Above All • Come, Now Is the Time to Worship • I Could Sing of Your Love Forever • More Precious Than Silver • Open the Eyes of My Heart • Shout to the Lord • and more.
00311207..$12.99

Complete song lists online at
www.halleonard.com

0719
060

World's Great Classical Music

This ambitious series is comprised entirely of new editions of some of the world's most beloved classical music. Each volume includes dozens of selections by the major talents in the history of European art music: Bach, Beethoven, Berlioz, Brahms, Debussy, Dvořák, Handel, Haydn, Mahler, Mendelssohn, Mozart, Rachmaninoff, Schubert, Schumann, Tchaikovsky, Verdi, Vivaldi, and dozens of other composers.

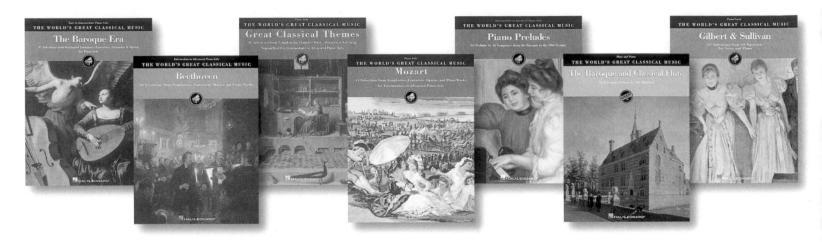

Easy to Intermediate Piano

The Baroque Era
00240057 Piano Solo $17.99

Beethoven
00220034 Piano Solo $15.99

The Classical Era
00240061 Piano Solo $15.99

Classical Masterpieces
00290520 Piano Solo $19.99

Easier Piano Classics
00290519 Piano Solo $16.99

Favorite Classical Themes
00220021 Piano Solo $18.99

Great Easier Piano Literature
00310304 Piano Solo $16.99

Mozart – Simplified Piano Solos
00220028 Piano Solo $16.99

Opera's Greatest Melodies
00220023 Piano Solo $18.99

The Romantic Era
00240068 Piano Solo $16.99

The Symphony
00220041 Piano Solo $14.95

Tchaikovsky – Simplified Piano Solos
00220027 Piano Solo $15.99

Intermediate to Advanced Piano

Bach
00220037 Piano Solo $16.99

The Baroque Era
00240060 Piano Solo $16.99

Beethoven
00220033 Piano Solo $15.95

Chopin Piano Music
00240344 Piano Solo $16.99

The Classical Era
00240063 Piano Solo $17.99

Debussy Piano Music
00240343 Piano Solo $17.99

Great Classical Themes
00310300 Piano Solo $15.99

Great Piano Literature
00310302 Piano Solo $18.99

Mozart
00220025 Piano Solo $14.99

Opera at the Piano
00310297 Piano Solo $16.99

Piano Classics
00290518 Piano Solo $17.99

Piano Preludes
00240248 Piano Solo $18.99

The Romantic Era
00240096 Piano Solo $16.99

Johann Strauss
00220035 Piano Solo $14.95

The Symphony
00220032 Piano Solo $16.99

Tchaikovsky
00220026 Piano Solo $15.99

Instrumental

The Baroque and Classical Flute
00841550 Flute and Piano $19.99

Masterworks for Guitar
00699503 Classical Guitar..................$16.95

The Romantic Flute
00240210 Flute and Piano $17.99

Vocal

Gilbert & Sullivan
00740142 Piano/Vocal........................$22.99

Prices, content and availability subject to change without notice.

HAL•LEONARD®

www.halleonard.com

0217